D0891781

# AMANA GRASS

*The Wesleyan Poetry Program: Volume 59*

# AMANA GRASS

BY

JON SILKIN

* * * * * * *

Wesleyan University Press

*Middletown, Connecticut*

Acknowledgments are due to:
BBC Poets Voice and Poetry Now; *The Blacksuede Boot; Borestone Mountain Poetry* (1967); *Choice; Form; The Iowa Defender;* Iowa State Liquor Store; *The Iowa Review; Journal of Creative Behaviour; Lines; Music & Arts* (Camden); *North American Review; North Now* (*Phamphlet No. 2*); *Northwest Review; Poetry & Audience; The Review; Scratch; Stand; Sumac; Times Literary Supplement.*

The "Killhope Wheel" group (excepting "Northumberland, for Instance" and "Poem") was first published by Midnag (Northumberland), 1971.

The Pym-Randall Press published the first three of "Six Cemetery Poems" in their pamphlet series as *Three Poems*, 1969.

"What are the lights, in dark, doing on water?" was first published by the *Massachusetts Review*, in 1968.

The title poem, "Amana Grass," was originally published in *The Iowa Review*, Volume I, number 1, 1970.

Paperback: ISBN: 0-8195-1059-9

Hardbound: ISBN: 0-8195-2059-4

Library of Congress Catalog Card Number: 71-153105

Manufactured in the United States of America

*First Edition*

"The bare declaration of political watchwords does not constitute political activity. On the other hand, the struggle of opinions as such, or the bringing about of certain changes in the social consciousness is political activity."

— *Othello and the Mangold-Wurzels*, by Andrzej Stawar
*Scrutiny*, Vol. VI, No. 1, June 1937, pp. 27–28

(Note on Stawar: a self-educated writer, was born at Warsaw in 1900, the son of a working man. His literary work began in 1924 with sociological and historical essays, and literary criticism. He [has] published articles on Marxism and art in 'left' literary journals, one of which, till its suppression, he edited. He has been in prison for his journalistic activities. — J. Needham)

"This spot is notorious for having been, for a long time, the residence of some runaway slaves, who, by cultivating a little ground near the top, contrived to eke out an existence. At length they were discovered, and a party of soldiers being sent, the whole were seized with the exception of one old woman, who, sooner than again be led into slavery, dashed herself to pieces from the summit of the mountain. In a Roman matron this would have been called a noble love of freedom; in a poor negress it is mere brutal obstinacy." — Darwin, *Voyage of a Naturalist*, Ch. II, p. 19
(OUP World's Classics)

*Contents*

✳



KILLHOPE WHEEL



✳

# SIX CEMETERY POEMS

In Iowa, we rested, seeing on a rib of ground behind a lighted field
a minute cemetery, without church. Flowers lie at the heads of
    lengths of turf
held motionless by the dead; flowers at the neckline of headstones
    chipped or not.
Of twenty, cared for, half were lopped, the material token
hacked where, below, the neckline was profusely tended.
Through cut grass roots of trees rise, at the surface burnished by feet,
    or by a roller.
The dead's place, combed here, and decked, by lively hands.
They are present, you said; why, if such force passes between your
    body and mine?
as the record plays, does your hand open my lips again?
what figures does the mirror keep
and the camera secrete of what the eye and it took?
These have died. I said: that woman remembers her daughter
quickened by her above ground.
I am not consoled, you said.
I want to keep your form which holds my flesh from bone to bone, open.
I am holding in me the breath of the dead; their breath, only.

From the road, I saw a small, rounded bluff, a cemetery
tufted on it, churchless, and squarely contained by wire fencing;
one more field, increasing in it a short, thick tree.
Its branches emerged, multiplying densely, compacting
an opaque bud of wood and leaves not chinking
light through, or air; populous of itself, impacted.
It had been planted among the dead, or grew
with them, first there perhaps, the dead
put about the tree, in urban grid-like plots.
Since void, that had tissue and bone from them disjoined
into bland nitrogens the tree burgeons in.
Burgeons and thickens, the graves tidied
emptily on its root-veined lumpy wildness;
the graves in distinguishable order,
their territorial bitterness lapsing
into the dense acid wood. Lingeringly
it darkens, and I feel the headstones' life
lengthening past the deads' lives, or any trim, lively care.
The stones split into the shape
the roots strain under with gregarious presence.
The fence's tension snaps, with the grid's.

he made the rampart and the wall lament;
they languished together

—*Lamentations* 2, viii

The face, in several sweet bones, fitted,
to her skull's, the bones shaped into its form, is fleshed
in joy
delighting in itself which issues joy, joyous to feel.
The hair congruous and abundant from pleasure springs
down her face to her knees, her legs folded beneath her, the hair, its
grieving length,
over the floor. I expect your cry.
A tree, as if its branches are of hair, bends
these, trailing them to its necessary pool. Stops there.
The hair of the tree fluxes to water.
Your hair, in branchfuls, the tree-shape
bends and flows through your face: the tree
in its all-eyed shape nurtured
by the untearful pool
shedding no jot of itself.
Where is the reciprocal shedding
from the faces, working in grief, the one for the other,
or between even you and me; your hurt
working its face from mine,
your tear in a metal-like
leaf, tugging, at the eye of him who'd weep, for the one weeping herself.
Nothing weeps here that does not weep, for itself, alone,
the tough small disc of grief
shuddering the body, the joyful hair leaping
like water to the ground in a cry.

In Anamosa sandstone is cut for a prison by men from Iowa.
Space fits where stone was, at its top a tree hangs its naked root through.
Below, they are sawing blocks; at the saw's teeth, nerves catch;
and skin, and hair at the fore arm, and dust congeal with sweat
a mucous not sensitive to its own touch. Slits in
the jail walls sense a division of light straiter than a chapel's.
As much width as the weeping judicial eye admits
of light at its mind. The prison honours the free men,
who work earth for corn. Here's a farm, a grain barn,
and at the limits of it, staked, a cemetery, every man
that is here on his feet. No weight of stone
keeps the man under earth, or headstone attributes
him. A stone column its head shrunk to it, a skull
bevelled and elongated, each as the next is, without
ornament, and no jot of name. No burial has been here,
earth cut, flesh wrapped, and the soil again heaped
on the flesh as though you felt it upon your own.
Each grave is uniform in the signification of death:
no grub hatches at where the flesh turns putrid, no smell
of flesh softly green insinuates the haired nostrils.
I feel the garb of each man's life, erect, obedient,
and stronger than the death of his body.

It has taken breath, but of that it seems to have none.
As though it had drawn breath and died, that, and its cage
    now, stiffened.
The grass bank swelled, is swelled and though rigid, is glad, an
    unadorned joy falling slowly across the incline,
that has yet being dead a winsome thing to offer.
On it neither flower nor beast, unless a man, treads
but in the rising, then flatness the slope bends into, mostly glad.
And at the crown, a house, not joyful, holds
in place that fluid continuous pleasure the ground
though dead does not hold back. As a man keeps
place with the peaceable, austere beasts he is disarmed by.
The house, in wood and white, shimmers, it dances
the government house, ample and consolidated, jigs—
in foreign substance timbered into American earth
various and fraternal. American Indians
dwindled into margins of plain flat under
bison with their bent horn the Indian must have,
that the white men bulleted. In Iowa
a cemetery is planted out and fenced on the town's margins,
square and strict, newish, the Jews', federated
as the wars demanded, or age did; the Jewish American
dead in earth, in rows, neat, decked with small limp flags.
In form, native; breathless, voided into the fecund
corn-belt, wanting memory: doctors, farm-men, dead soldiers
merged with clart particles of soil
that can't grasp spaces until wormed
by flesh that's American, dead, preponderant
and exalted. The others are scattered
boneless, and wearied of their individual substance
blent and lost near the cemented onrush of crank-ridden highway,
the fast interstate mindfully pressed
between two steep flanks of heavy soil,
one dwindling slowly to the cemetery, a loose iron gate to it,
foundling, amnesiac, the most recent.

for Paul Tracy

Miners dead inside coal seamed by fire, under Pittsburgh
or between lead, from poison that touched and made stiff
the liver as it opened last: what the flesh failed of
employment caused. Prospectors, their wives, and issue
come of wiving, they are each dead
who obsessed, impregnated, and made the retina
gravid with images of silver.
I found evidence of them on a hill below
where the cage had ceased; no church by them, or metal.
I found more dead, fewer though, near a canyon
named Sucker Creek, east from that, and in
a field, the green square it contained staked with posts
erect at the corners, holding wire up.
Few dead, where few were living, and against
their solitary gentleness, or brutality, as some
fetched a tendon to their neighbours' throats, a farm cart
with four large wheels, its shafts erect, dark red
and stiff above the wire its carcase
is tethered at; living carcase; the arms
raised in astonishment, and fixed
at joints stuck now. Perpetually agape.
Together, the dead are crustacean, the large
crab of the soil, pincering its track under
earth that will fracture, webbed by micturating roots
dregging earth of its nutriment. The dead heave it open
and move with vulnerable hugeness on it.
A four legged slowness that is a limp almost.
I hear each ligament and tendon working
to print back on us what we let them have
as they aged and sickened; I am afraid

of the jointed, vulnerable, crab-wise dead.
The cemetery waits, contemptuously patient
at their congealed practice. Listless crust about soft flesh.
The cart's arms jar, their load to be re-assumed.

AMANA GRASS

## *Amana Grass*

The leaf of your hand shall touch but not cover me
—*New England Proverb*

Amana grass, its spikes of hair rayed as branches
from long stems, is sucked by three locomotives, their haul
filling space over tracks. Wind wraps its length,
hot and dieseled, through spaces of stumpy grass, barely green
over long slight inclines. Air in varying pressures blowing on the train
sounds fiercely between houses, where space, holding
other spaces, of human loneliness, meshes.
The same in that wildness locomotives haven't seen;
beneath earth filaments of root, everything, tangle.
The train links points in which the human crouches,
is found, rejoices. Wind appears to feel out crevice,
and surface. Does not feel, no pain at all in how it contacts.
The sun's light, without visible sun, sinks coldly through frigid wind.
A leaf turns upon asphalt treading through the park.
Wind picks at a face rising and sinking on long legs
stockinged, their tan rushing to compare with the net's colour.
Nearing, she seems to compose her face, the air being frigid.
Slim, as the legs are, almost a woman's; not fleshy yet, or coy now
the thighs swelling behind a skirt now short, the hips
larger than they were, composed, each, into tentative prominence
the mild fury she receives of her intent frail hulk.
Of the mid-west, in bulk, solemn, a flat grandeur under its heights of corn,
she strains little to her. Of what is there,
a train's horn contracting desolating space.
Of what she is, something ribbed; of what she has, nearing,
the rib enlarged. Of who she'll be,
the clasp that broaches two minds, hasn't enjoined them.
The face's sadness, tenacious shadow, melts into resolution.
Speak louder; shout, for I should hear,

the wind asks, each creature begged of it.
Each thing is to its need, not much remaining to implore.
Space the train threads grasps for more; in it, a tree
shakes leaves rustlingly at grasses naming them sharp stump.
Grass tightens fierce roots on fractions of soil.
The soil, from stone, in passivity, grins; is to ingest all.
How, among nature's divine egotisms, to grow
her especial fronds, antennae sensible to another.
To enlarge, amid these natures, whose heraldic egotisms silently conflict,
she must fight. Earth's fulness, though,
may be shared; fleshy needs, feathery demands, requited
"among the stained emblems under which the stiffened flesh
fragments. On the bits, vultures perch that, gleaming
on frozen blood as if armour mirroring the dead enemy's conquest,
rip the flesh
their image flares on, captive since to what they strip,
flesh, not stubborn or curious." Brown grass ends are as limp,
and thinned, as crystals of falling snow are intense:
experienced and dense, the aged spirit sheds itself.
Appear in the air, edged; bitter against nostrils and cheekbone.
Wind stirs it onto each creature unremembering of earlier needs
to be requited by what creeps and grins against its knots.
She tightens her coat onto her breasts, scarf lightly to her ears.
She'll get home. He moves through it, sure he'll find her;
white powders, some of heaven's properties, sift over the sidewalk
bonily cramping the foot inside its strict shoe.
Treading he sees in virgin snow someone's feet printed
towards her house, before him, his, exactly. Snow
lifts into his face, melting flakes caught in clenched eyelashes,
blasted on edge to him it is adrenalin charging
the mind's eye to dilate over the prints. Calmness
then. He turns, from tracked eddies of feet past
her house, to her, feeling for her ornate small key.
The evening star, in fruitful magnificence, rises with moistening splendour,

towards the sky's taut, precise limits.
He approaches, the counterpane unpuckered, smooth for the crushing of
heedless, fruitful weight.
No evening meal. Thought of food prepared by each one
broken down, as if by enzyme, into other hunger.
Pancakes nurtured into floury presence; stay-in-bed hash; sauce
biting its butterscotchings sweetly into cream and cake; these, gone.
Her lips parted as if breath, passing between, stirred the loose hair shaking
past the forehead,
she summons the first kiss to her body. He parts her lips, his tongue
stiffened into her.
The spirit dilates; the fleshy circlet starts its flow.
Older, he prepares: on his breast heraldries of self-power
chevalring love
stain him: on her breasts, prints of the stain.
He presses her down, she helping him, parts her, and enters.
She won't move. Forced to him, and pinned, she can't.
The spike piercing the belt that holds it as it stiffens
upon the bar; tightened upon each other:
so he in her, so she round him. Malely and femalely
they are clung by self-swellings they can't slip
of a sexual love ending each other's
mirroring vauntedness. 'For whom do I brag?'
Then stricken to tenderness, minted, as if to the doe's hunter,
he asks of her: 'Did we make this, of our intent hungers?'
She fears it may be worse. She, feeling pure, the dew might look
sullied. The purities in her chill, condensing her heat
to drops that lustre her success, or, if she fails, rebuke her
that she melted in her their dewy script that
in unsweatlike nature gleams through the skin of women.
He gets off her, hot and distanced; she faces up to the ceiling;
her thighs are separate in distress and coldness.
Flat Iowa is stretched in snow, through which her Vermont hills rise
strict as her mother's breast, wrinkling the torn flats they break.

Her nipples lose their stiffness, her breasts not thickening a milk
should have milk were a hand on them, be smaller than his.
A strict, sweet whiteness, purely of her breasts
is, for her, the milk achingly sucked by her child's lips.
Unlike her vaginal whitenesses, or a man's sperm, flukelike
at her itch; her breasts' exclusion, each one.
He turns from position onto his back. Wind like pricking metal
over the surface of another exclaims a passion
length-like as the scoring on him of hair naked.
Like the pressure of touch, the wind's, her hair scrapes her silence
through him its length. It is to him as to a beast
that working four he puts a hundred feet down
to his mile of hillside's inch.
Her silence teases her apart, forming distance, cars
slithering from each other. She separate, he distanced.
It is England's width, soon, the north part, stone,
where the silver mine fills, on chipped quartz, chipped limestone,
earth, wire,
lies, at any rate, choked,—the plants at this segment of earth's carefully
spun rim
rubbed small, low, wiry, red; car-rush whirring such colour
rearward of the mind, darkening, with the sun
melting
through north England, its heights, flat as Iowa's,
dark, extinct, which he travels.—As she moves away
to Vermont's hills, shrunk, folding as they cooled
into claustral heights, wooded though, familial.
The New England heart is contracted in virtue
durably
to itself; as a mistress to her heart's blood-holding loneliness
attaches herself. The ancient stems of plants
dilate to water's ancient tractability,
averting our care. 'Haven't we, at least,' he asks
'nurtured each other?' 'Yes' she replies 'and been weaned

off each other. I have. Although you, I see, still
think of us as creatures, creatures or plants, in symbiosis.
I want nothing. I mean, I want purely
on my own, strengthening my especial substance
to grow itself,—a plant thickens its xylem
from water for more of it.'
Her strength, a boiling fluid,
wells to her vessel's brim; she spills not a dram
through hatred's surface.
'Why bear with me? Haven't I hurt enough
what once I seemed to value?' He feels tenderness,
as if excremental, evacuated from her.
She feels herself a mountain creature, exalted to the permanence
of the rock-born species. At the door she backs onto
she asks: 'Am only I culpable, or are you
some guilty creature also?' 'It's as though,' he answers
'your strength laments of itself, or the attent
sinew finds 'no' what most charges it.'
'Isn't that what you want?' she asks. 'I want more,'
he answers her, 'as you do.' 'Then want's
our portion.' 'Need it be?' he questions.
'My attention makes small, yes and lucid the plenitude of us,
the water-seeming fall of hair, gathered, then braided to a gleaming length
seamlessly twined, into an image feelings breathe themselves in,
value insists on, until memory fixes, prints and shows as experience.'
'That's not like experience,' she recoils. 'It may
be how it works, but how it works is theory,
and I want the thing, and want it mine.'
'We're not machines,' he goes on, 'and how we work
is how we value what works in us.'
'I don't have value'; Her hair glowers
on her copper skin, anvil and substance, clashed
into hissing and cooled re-formation.
'Listen,' he says; the space between them pauses:

'when your mother had you and you were pressed
through the tract a stranger to her womb had eagerly before approached,
after you left, with a body of wrinkled skin
and no more, except for the initiation of breath,
as if for breath, you turned to your lung-like past.
Of anything gracious, firm there, and mild, didn't you add
the sinew, flexions and tendernesses, you and I
had from each other; your mind with such light from this
in your skin it gleamed, lustring the undewlike sweat
that from your body's heat expressed your shape, stilling you.
In that decent stillness we did nothing that day.
As though over the moss, each plant, each flower, we lay between
fitted the intent self to a peaceable kingdom, toxic leaves
and petals, by lively consent, being sucked
of poisons by elements they had with care selected,
and compounded into wrathful and frigid bitterness.
It was consent. So it seemed to us
in the vacant wilderness.

                                        Your eyes shut
in concentration, mine alerted through me
a wakeful quiet . . . '

                                        —'That may be so,' she said
stepping from the door.

                                        This, this reduces to the nub

                                                                        events
through a tumid spring to mid winter;

                                                        the thorn,
with sporadic sheen, budding in the mid-west's spaces,
the lustre against such nature. Wildness
abhors space filled unless more brims it;
Physics denies, wrongly, in this case.
This is not a love poem to do with love, not,
what goddesses of love exact, for love, of their gods:

the complex swelling of bud and root, crossings of branch and leaf;
nor in fiery points synoptic verse, distanced, entailed,
with sensibility at the fingers' ends, in men's folly.
It is not, either, verse for someone; though a poem
of love I experienced, whose image is troubled
in America's: brutal, shankered; a magnificence
of Roman cloth umbering an Etruscan shade.
With vital parts, also, touched with self-doubt. And still,
the following lists of attributes, in this disorder:
fearful, isolated: what men cancerously die of.
What more to bite on? What is more than enough,
what is in plenty, in the widths we congregate,
of estate, insurance, its probity—or else
the unassailable defection from honesty—
isolates, or aligns our sly feelings,
at our circuits, pinched into our chosen
antipathy or liking. The intrinsic being perishes.
An animal keeps his passion; we aren't of them.
Perhaps I can tease of this plenty nothing; not of America.
So that of the two, of this single image
in two metaphors, love is rendered, that gracious abstract
passing through the naked upright fork
of hell and heaven, scathed, through that quaint background,
but, now, advancing. And since witchery,
the sapphired and webbed flesh of angels
is now unseen against the sky, elements
of love tinged with fire and pasture loosen
annealed unearthly cries
as rigorous spirit for our earthly needs.
I have never controlled it, a quadrant
I am an interval of. 'Love' I cried
once, 'love', between the markings,
and was quiet; with little before that
to say, though it comes now. It presses me

to revalue what is in obedience to me
and think of control, again, its limitations
its constant limitations, against openness.
I must know that something like you is alive still,
something quick, something tense at its quick, at the quick,
alert, and with that, making the sinew bright and sharp,
the whole tendon and muscle on the bone with no
hint at death, or scent, or thing like that.
I must know that there is no death on you; that of you
more beauty stares than in your image.
Therefore you shall stay alive. I need clarity.
I need the image of you bearable
by control, and within my courage;
or my courage to grow, matching that quick in you
paying out the veined, the thin, lines
of your shape in durable contour.
But that is exacting. So the thing I want
is that you with the passionate elegance of a beast
into the man's love breathe yours; in age, holding
your value to your body, move, as you must,
in some reluctance, to your death.
—A night past I dreamt of the hire purchase man
asleep with his wife; both seemed young and pliant.
They lay naked; his arms clasping her waist,
his head rested between her supple breasts.
I saw that he dreamt, and what it was; and that
not of his wife, or of some other deeply
moulded eager girl. Belshazzar-like
he dreamed that, fanged, he, on hands and knees, crept
with open salivating jaws on the poor
and negroes, lively victims, in his right hand
the papers of his wealth-to-be laced
with the strictures, bonds, enforcements that would ligament
them to him. His wife stood naked

and grinning among us, papering the ink-smeared
visible body with signed bonds,
but mostly, about her cunt, she pressed
the papers, wadding and girding her fruitful organs,
shutting her sex from view, and access. This was
her assent, her husband's dream, and my containment.
I was speaking of love, and America; and how
I value it, as I knew you did,
when you wrote: 'I want to be a woman
to a man so badly, I can taste it almost.'
I was speaking of value, I guess. Of what
knits in the spaces, where wind
creases its frigid movements into the face
as it swerves on. I was speaking of you,
and of love once more: warm, intelligenced, exacting;
of more immanent value than Hebrew parallelism
or the Anglo Saxon metre.

## *A Word about Freedom and Identity in Tel-Aviv*

Through a square sealed-off with
a grey & ornate house,
its length bent, for one corner of that,
a road leads off, got to down steps:
wide, terraced, ample.
The road's quiet, too; but nudges as
the square did not. Walking
some below the city I heard
a pared, harsh cry, sustained
and hovering, between outrage
and despair; scraped by itself
into a wedge-shape opening on
inaccessibly demented hurt
it can't since quite come at;
imitative, harsh, genuine.
A pet-shop four feet below
pavement level; in its front yard
a blue parrot, its open beak
hooked and black, the folded wings
irregularly lifting a little;
under which, dull yellow, soft plumage,
the insides of itself, heaved, slightly.
Its tail was long, stiff. Long in stiffness
that at once bends entirely
if bent too much. And as it
turned in its cage, bending the tail
against the wires, it spoke
into the claw it raised
at its hooked face, the word
'toràh, toràh' in the hoarse, devotional
grief religious men speak with
rendering on God the law

their love binds them with. Done,
it cried its own cry, its claws tightening
onto its beak, shaking slowly
the whole face with the cry
from side to side. This cry was placed
by one Jew inside another. Not belonging though;
an animal of no distinct race,
its cry also human, slightly;
wired in, waiting; fed on
good seed a bit casually
planted. Granulated, sifted,
dry. The toràh is:
suffering begets suffering, that is.

(The Toràh consists of the body of Jewish religious knowledge.)

## *Reclaimed Area*

Walking up sands, offal is gaped from a tunnel seaward, muddying its edge.
Bowels ceaselessly open, add to the sea, not much. Broken tackle drifts
up, shored. The sea sucks off noisefully. Many pieces sprawl
each like the carapace of an insect bent open and then made flat.
Concrete slabs improperly founder in sand. A brick.
A way between stone is pressed by the hot foot flat, although dry. The
    sand ends.
A boot disconsolate of its wearer. Mourns him. Nothing mourns. Each thing
is individual and broken. The fresh sea is impounded by sewage, bordering
a domain where refuse in such profusion grows the eye is astonished at the
    potents of men.
It's all battered. You go over it, straight. A road starts
with houses on it of the English Mandate: substantial
walls fortressed against heat. Some windows pointedly
shaped for the Arabs: a concession. The Arabs are ruled again,
not by the Turkish mind, this one, a flower with petals spiked, broad,
sharp, bashed out of a sword and planted, has displaced the earlier—
was tempered in the north. Some houses have broken; others, partly.
Washing sweats. Peel, stalk, pot all lifted to the sweeper's barrow.
The road is pared to its soil, scraped to where the ant
eats in bent and long-legged splendour, having our waste
or not, as the broom lets it. Further, at the town's focus
coffee is tipped into the mouth, lips gripping the glass.
No wrinkle, or flexion from it returns the darkening pressure of the lip.
The mouth affords the town's prices; skin is regarded for its texture.
Waste from here mingles with the others', bowelled into the sea.
The ant from omniverous takings distills
its formic acid to bite with as its unregarded jaws grow.

## *Jaffa, and Other Places*

Toward Jaffa, foot-dragged sand is flattened, and pathed, the hardened
    grains
fusing then to a road, on which the fallen foot stifles. Houses shake
    into dereliction.
A flat incohering of sand with brick, remaining feet above, stays.
A gulley cuts through these levels down, sprains in its sides, between
which pours brick, charred wood, tarpaulin, stopped. Inertia heaps:
mound of boots, motionless and brown, remains of the mandate army,
    dispersed in England now.
Done with in worse places: shoes, crutches, irons, many oddments, each
    similar, the inert teeth, ash, hair, dust
winnowed between grains of soil or not winnowed between them;
most of each category useful, separated. The flesh gets isolated from these,
the goods and its body harrowed apart. Each item heaps on
one of its kind, itself buried. Wardresses help sort each class.
And not the negro, his hunted skin finding each shadow not as dark as he
offers an absence as blank. Shortly the spider
is trained to bite at the organ; the bone round it liquifies, the lips
of it attendant and limp. The Reich's swollen architecture will be less dank.
New immigrants near this ashy zone, pacified and burnt.

What are the lights, in dark, doing on water?
That is fishermen, intruding nets
sifting into, and pulling from, in pairs.
Lights, also; fixed on boats that
in moorings heave of water tugged by a soft moon.
All cheese; while fish squirm in hundreds.
There's a fear in that light giving
the bleak water a foot, at least, of green and depth.
That's excellent for sight; in it
the mind shakes, working out one thing,
known; and the other distracting it
from being so. I know what the men do;
what if, precisely, they aren't doing it.
In darkness, light opens the eye
as the eye opens a distance out.
Though not at all. It only seems to.
How if they only seem to strike
nets for fish; the fish go on perishing.
Lord God, I am afraid.
Then better. Speaking on you I
feel comforted you're not at all.
Not, that means, at all.
Although, I still can't tell
if these men are doing what
they seem to me to. You will
tell me, love, if you seem loved.
A long time, I leant on myself,
the stick, short. You are quite near now.
Tell me it is you that's reached into by me
and not by you, as I delivered myself to me.
And yet, please explain, quite slowly,
why it is that, giving love but which the other
incorporates only slowly, that then the other
becomes distinct; and why it is the force

you are the nakedness of
gives us clarity. Perhaps
you can say why. Or I'll put
my hands under you again

## *Conditions*

Shabbat: the sun is slithering into earth, now; the molten tip
of a pole, searching; the synagogues open; renewing
its heat detached in the earth's; from that, a ruby smelts.
The synagogues light, redly. Off one,
a room, its volumes half the size of a man, erect. Does God
live between spaces defined in the Hebrew script crushed upright?

So much oblivion in
such librarianship.

Part of me feels as though
it would like to believe.
Care for after death
seems a balm swathed over the terrorful
body that, with life,
was beautiful as a god;
its fluxing gleams resemble
the wick that constantly
sheds with its lightful wax
their immortality.

Three conditions diverge
their singularity.

Comradeliness, where terror
at death is sprung into
a thread, stretched to fixed points,
staked, where each friend stands.
The thread that's stretched absorbs
the other's tremoring.
It burns along itself;
it is the news that one

constantly sheds from him.

The second is death, which cramps
each creature in his pain,
and is joy's measurement.
Both seem gifts of one
divine, offered up to death,
which is the flame exacting
the tallow and cord into
their own magnificence
and an extinction shrunk
under a flat, black vault;
as in exchange, the fixed
remedial care of God.

The third condition is where
a man sees by his flame
whose dark he shrinks into.
And each gout of permanence
is used, charred extinct.
I feel some terror here.
The small individual pool
of tallow hardening in death.
And taken in the lump
nothing much comforts it.
Or taken, anyhow.
Courageous, animal.
Melted with others' lives
into a wax flame of
a small magnificence.

## *Ayalon*

Let the sun stop
Let the moon stand still

They have halted, sun and moon, lit
and congruent on us, and discover
the smutch granuled where tissue
crept together and healed.

They have halted: no thought
has clothing;
the hair of her flesh cannot help if it is seen.

It is seen, it is seen
that an Arab village its Arabs left
Jews brought explosives to.
The stone lit against each seam, and clasp
where the fluid silica, developing privacy,
rippled and set

as if the olive stone were opened on a meticulous nut-like seed
white between the fingers

a baleful spike grazed the fine, dismal stone.

May the eyelid be a curse until now, but may no further sleep,
or what passes for it,
let the nerves ponder
in a skein upon the bone.

The moon with a
swab of cold.

She and he are to move as we were grown to them.
Their light needs us,
decked, restored and lively
with each other; and we
the periodicity of the eyelid
drooping
over the lashless eye.

## *Bull-god*

The earth's not round at all
it holds no poles flattened to it:

a bull-god. The haunched-up limbs,
not bothered any, flex clankingly against
a rigid stomach, at the testes poised
for rut. A clinkered heaviness. The head
is groomed, hair of it and face kempt and woven
making the face smile with huge moist power.
As religious Jews wear it, their hair though not as thick
which coils and hangs. His hair is their conqueror's.
And the wings, nilish green come
of blood of the river's reptiles expressed into a scale,
stiffen us, nightly, into them. By day we scrape
and irritate the unearthly shard-like integument
into substance that we'd have with moisture, as dry clods.
Trees rise to the diameter of a hair.
Night folds again, as wings, screening together
the light pressed between them, corrugating it.
The moon, lit, has been glimpsed; it is much
incompetent grappling to cover, wrap
her cold thighs in translucency.
Her unhappiness is a cold swab, internally nursed,
a perpetual thin white menstruation
by rote faithful to childlessness.
We have none of her eking light, wings
about our crouched forms in Babylonian ribbing
vault our soft-shelled glowing flesh.
The impish grin of the dead, white-skinned
succour their malice on us. There, in the earth, there,
through it, I mean, their faces emerge, or through
the mineral veined, white flesh of others

dead, they smile. Smiling, the matted square beard
hardens in its sleek undulatings. The dead here,
and other than here, in their spiritual progress
deflect the material offering some make
of the obsolete piastre lustring its worth
upon them. Stamped both sides, without head on either.
Much immunity serves these dead; for us it assembles
in us, the living, a stone in us in our organs
that they were once like us.

## *Divisions*

Cedars from Lebanon, in community, move into the swart, pointed hills.
I don't say many. On two legs bound into one,
rooted into terraces between drops of rock-face, in sparse soils
cornered where wind pushed that. Layers of snapping pointed stone shift,
one can guess, like whelpings, about their roots.
These roots know what they are about. The trees came together; tall,
    fleshed like a wax feather,
their leaves green throughout. And as the sun changes the trees don't;
    sharp, slim.
Not many know what sex these creatures are made of.
The whole tree comes into the folded integral hills
of Judah, one of many, towards a sea struggling
to erode from the land its form into the shape of Africa.
Creatures with two legs come, and sit against a Cedar that no longer moves
forward. They spread a map over their legs, engross a frontier;
a document embossed by lines that divide one bit of land from the same bit,
the first of these trees from the last of them. The line is
arbitrary as a fish-hook. As if two iron hooks
stuck like picks into the ground, and their shafts pulled,
until in the earth a gap opened. A small, neat structure of stones,
in fact, marks the hostile step which it is death to step.
Judah's hills do not stoop, they are said to skip; those trees
in Lebanon do not bend; their mild, emulsive
sharpnesses advance through the nourishing earth they compact.
A hexagon of dirt is trapped back by a leaf into the soil.
Suddenly the landscape, one might say, is startled by
a man in a blue shirt, its greens, its ochres fixed by a depth of blue;
as if before these changed but now were frozen by the quality of blue
    that they are not.
He crouches; what is he speaking to the wrinkled olive; what disdain
for the tree's agedness as the plucked creature furs its oil on his salt fingers?
The hills shimmer; also, the trees standing in them: a trembling on one

point from inside. A haze, in dots, condenses over the contracted earth.
Past that tree, there, that shorter one, two men are dead.
The sun is pushing off, the trees persist inside their shade
eating deeply on the earth. Opening the clothes you see
among the groiny hair, the useful penis, in the heat distended slightly.
One of the men's has a head, circumcised; a chin, a ridge
that visibly hardened as its body's blood gathered to it intently.
Alive, a bit of marble with a ruff of skin, in folds; thin, brown, slack.
The other man's is hooded. Each had its fissure that as it entered it
the lips folded back upon themselves, the ground moistening its entrance.
Now the vulva, slightly swollen, its hair local, remains closed however.
The lips closed, in a pained sleep: the female part ruminant.
No: the female part mourns the unique instrument it was to it.
The faces of the men show that death, which each divided on the other's
body, entered the left ear, and then the mouth. In leisure.
None attends them. The sabbath intervenes like a blade.

## *Worm*

Look out, they say, for yourself.
The worm doesn't. It is blind
As a sloe; its death by cutting,
Bitter. Its oozed length is ringed,
With parts swollen. Cold and blind
It is graspable, and writhes
In your hot hand; a small snake, unvenomous.
Its seeds furred and moist
It sexes by lying beside another,
In its eking conjunction of seed
Wriggling and worm-like.
Its ganglia are in its head,
And if this is severed
It must grow backwards.
It is lowly, useful, pink. It breaks
Tons of soil, gorging the humus
Its whole length; its shit a fine cast
Coiled in heaps, a burial mound, or like a shell
Made by a dead snail.
It has a life, which is virtuous
As a farmer's, making his own food.
Passionless as a hoe, sometimes, persistent.
Does not want to kill a thing.

## *Creatures*

Shells are now found
Of creatures not still subsisting,
Chipped from the hardened mud under
Which oil lurks.

Men came with their chipped diamonds
And a pole with these smelted onto it
To bore rock. Oil broke out
Into the clear American air.

Barely noticed at the time
Among the soil screwed from
Above the crude useful oil,
Shells, about half an inch.
They were whorled, and chipped from
What they had been hardening in,
Falling through the glistening mud
They filled with; the spiral
Wriggling creature gone from them.
It is a spiral horn, silent;
And shaped like an inert
Clammy-skinned spring.

They grew property:
An amnion, a house;
Their grave no more special,
No more particular than
A pattern, a repetition of curving
Continuous shape, for survival.

## *Flatfish*

1

It moves vertically through salted
Pressures, with a head that sees sideways.
The nets are submerged, which it enters.
Nothing to come for specially. Men want it.

The white flesh powered by a tail filmed with skin
Sways its mild hulk into their fold.
The white flesh is food. When boiled,
It flakes easily off the bone.

Is this love? God created us
For the toothed shark, the molestation
Of two jaws hinged through flesh
Onto each other's hooked teeth.

Its ethics are formal, determined.
Otherwise He made the mild flatfish,
And gleaning mackerel that fatten
On the dead's helplessness strengthening its rancid colours.

He made the flatfish, their eyes
Naive as a bead drawn from a leopard's skin.
Their white flesh is flaked into the mossy,
Acidic belly, just hanging.

The good salt, phosphate, each dissolved
Into flesh. The fish are left to gasp
In ships' holds, mulcting the air
For air moving in the gill's membrane

Miserly, useless. A gradual pain
Until the fish weaken. Could they cry
We might gas them to concert
Their distress. Nets are men's media,

Their formal, knotted, rectangular intelligence.
They survive on what the fish weighs, their welfare
Accurate as a pair of scales.

2

    We are not going to change.
But husband the sea, planting the fish spawn in
        The frigid heft of plot-water
            Grey, but not stone.

    Mackerel will gorge
A sea parsley, its flowers sprinkled with a white, granular petal;
        The shark will eat mud
            At the sea's foundation.

    Though to reap will be by net,
As many fish as grains husked from their flattened case,
        The ear raped of its oval bolus
            Folded into itself.

    The precise allotment of fish
A growth in kind; pollination by a brush tasked
        Onto differing species
            For the flesh's good.

    The flesh's good. Elsewhere
We seized on our own kind, not for food. Each fish

Glides through a forest,
An oily lung

Of sea weed, the swell
Moved in a land-grafted integument of sea plant. A uniform
Thicket moon-masted, its foliage
Begins to lock

Fast with sea-forester's
Skill. We evolve with our hands and brain. The pad of each
Hand, moist; the nails sharp
As a grown fin.

# KILLHOPE WHEEL

*Tree*

Under the yard, earth could enable nothing, nothing
opened in it. I smelt it once, when the floor
was up, disabled, rank. I made boxes
and grow mint, rhubarb, parsley
and seedlings that lift a furl of leaves, slightly
aside an unwavering stem.
A friend dragged a barrel off rocks, we took it home;
I chose a tree for it. It is five foot
with branches that may stretch across
the wall, with minute fruits, of hardly any colour.
Its leaves point open, and down. The whole tree
can glisten, or die. It is dark green
in earth mixed with peat dug by a lake
and dung I crumbled in.
I can't fudge up a relationship, but it gladdens
you, as the sun concentrates it, and I
want the creature for what it is
to live beyond me.

Small hills, among the fells, come apart from the large
where streams drop; the water-flowers
bloom at the edges, or in the shallows, together,
and are white. Whoever comes here, comes, glad, at least
and as they look, it is with some care, you can feel
that on flower, may tree, or dry-stone wall
their gaze collects in a moist, comely pressure.
I feel this, but slog elsewhere.
Swan Hunter's is where we build naval craft;
they emerge: destroyer, the submarine
fitted, at length, by electricians. Their work
is inspected; it is again re-wired. In the heat
men walk high in the hulk on planks, one
of them tips, and he falls the depth of the hold.
It is hot. The shithouses are clagged, the yard's
gates closed for security. The food is not good.
Some people in here are maimed.
I am trying to make again the feeling
plants have, and each creature has, looked at,
demure, exultant. The man who has fallen
looks at me, and looks away

## *Northumberland, for Instance*

The stream's tributary depth is thin
flint at the bed, flint's casting heat burnt
in its splinters in smoky, frigid rings.

In chill unextinguishable water.

And over it, a bridge
mounded on two jambs forming an arch, no door; its feet
in talons gripping
shallow, evasive water.

They don't. That aimless clarity
funnels mindlessly between
a gap-clawed power. Not between villages: links
serves and remembers. Is its lord's power.
And is shafted in the gregarious effort
of two hands and a back in one muscle
of several men. Several men
made this new bridge, the road bowed
up in concrete, each of its feet
twelve seconds apart. Being boneless,
it has the sinew of many worked into it,
fluid and tendon filamented into it.
The first bridge is heraldic; the beasts of the master
struck into his sign in virtue of their strength.

The bridges straddle water; and crossing
either, we are
permitted: by who built them

and are each a colony
in stone glaciated into
each other

who would be contributary, a distinct
step, a curve, a heave of laughter of itself

*Centering*

At the West End, a bridge.
Coaling houses, shutes, and among such power,
contrived, at the top, a little lever
which would unclasp the heavy trap.
All the ships come for here is fuel. Few come.
And none, further.
Near the bridge, each side, houses
struggling to cross over.

More east, seawards, a further bridge.
The trains bend that way, then, turning square,
cross the whole river.
Below, the quay, meant to focus
activity to it.

The maritime offices, craft
moored from Denmark.
The masts' shadows stable on the customs sheds.

No centre can be formed
here or by the next bridge. The trains
pass on a tier above the road.

Nor here; the road belts between
the strength of the region fused into two spans,
gone.

Two precipitate banks, where water pushes
within a moment of the quick of you, bituminous
and rank.
If you were made
at the river-side
you have to be a spanning, at least.

*Killhope Wheel*
*1860*
*County Durham*

1860. Killhope Wheel, cast
forty feet in iron across, is swung
by water off the North Pennines
washing lead ore crushed here.

And mined, here. Also fluor-spar.
In 1860 soldiers might kill
miners if they struck.

A board says that we're free to come in.
Why should it seem absurd to get
pain from such permission? Why have

I to see red coat soldiers prick
between washed stones, and bayonets
tugged from the seeping flesh?

Among the north pennines what might
have opened the flesh of miners, who chucked
their tools aside?

I can't work out what I have
come here for; there's no mineable lead
or work of that kind here now.

Why does a board, tacked to wood,
concerning my being free to visit
give my useless pain nourishment?

Like water. I am its water, dispersed

in the ground I came from; and have footage
on these hills, stripped of lead,

which the sheep crop, insensibly white.
The mist soaks their cries into them.

## *Strike*

The earth comes moist-looking, and blackens;
a trickle of earth where the feet pressed,
twice a day, wearing off the grass.
Where the miners
were seen: a letter blown damply
into the corner of a hut: "Oh dear love, come to me"
and nothing else.

Where are they?
The sheep bleat back to the mist balding
with terror; where
are they? The miners
are under the ground.

A pale blue patch of thick worsted
a scrag of cotton;
the wheel is still that washed the pounded ore.
They were cut down.

Almost turned by water, a stammer of the huge wheel
groping at the bearings.
Their bayonets; the red coat
gluey with red.
The water shrinks
to its source. The wheel,
in balance.

## *Spade*

George Culley, Isaac Greener?

A want of sound hangs
in a drop of moisture from the wheel that
turned and washed the ore.

A rustling of clothes on the wind. The water does not move.

I have come here to be afraid.
I came for love to bundle
what was mine. I am scared
to sneak into the hut to find your coat.

When you put down your pick,
when others wouldn't sprag
the mine's passages; when you said no:

soldiers, who do not strike,
thrust
their bayonets into you.

They were told to.

The young mayor, shitting, closeted
with chain on his neck. I want to

push my hands into your blood
because I caused you to use yours.

I did not die; love, I did not. All the parts
of England fell melting like lead away,

as you showed me the melting once, when you and the men
with you were jabbed,

and without tenderness, were filled over;
no psalm, leaf-like, shading the eyelid
as the eye beneath is dazed abruptly
in the earth's flare of black light
burning after death.

The spade digging in the sunlight illuminates the face of my God.
Blind him.

Concerning strength,
it is unequal. In a paddock
by Stakeford, slag, with bushes dripping
over stone, a horse crops, slowly, his strength
tethered into the ground. The Wansbeck
shivers over the stone, bits of coal, and where
it halts a pool fills, oily
and twitching. Closer to the sea, it drops
under a bridge, coming to ground
where the mind opens, and gives uselessly to
the sun such created heat the air
cleaves to the flesh,
the bench facing the water, sat on by old men.
If this goes, nothing: this clearness
which draws a supple smell through old skin
making a pause for it. Houses and scrap will heap,
and flake, as
if organs of the soil clagged
with shreddings of rust.

## *Platelayer*
(for J.M.)

'I did not serve, but was skilled
for fifty years, laying plates
measured as carefully apart
as seedlings.' The line came
west from Morpeth, crossing
the third road for Scotland.
At Knowesgate, four houses
group on a bank, set away.
A station was built there.
'I laid plates for eight miles,
but short of Morpeth, sledging chucks
that held the rails; kept them so,
although this has gone now.
Yet here are four pines of
the five I put in. And here
I helped to concrete that
that was the goods bay.
My dog has sixteen years.
We both suffer the heat.
And yet her owners had said
that she must be put down.
I did not say that. And the lupins
strike through the platform;
with a better chance they'd have not
done well, I think.
But what I think is that
my work was finished up: five years
past the track taken apart.
No, not so; now we've cranes
to hoist the lengths that we
laid down, form on form. Also gone

a certain friend, who finished
when I was made free.
I shan't work any job
twice. And this is strange,
having the letter from the man,
although it was not him.
Yet surely as like him
as the bolts drove in.
"I can't think of your name
or what you are. You must
excuse me and I have
nothing to tell you and
why I am shut up here
I can't speak of with nothing
to speak about."
But still I am certain
the track we built was skilled,
although you can't tell that.'

## *Poem*

At Laggan, iron
bridges the Spey's banks, water
on these, snowed. By Dalthoilly though
Spey braids into a small loch
again closing on a clump of homes.
Bridged with concrete, then, the road marches
ranking trees keep the earth soft and pine-smelling.
Light crosses the earth. We come out
between higher walls, of mountain white
as with sky, that shelf indistinguishable
in white; the black gaps glower.
From the bare peak bluish light
tilts, where life isn't, showing upwards
each facet assured and monstrous
of bent and pointed squareness.
Wind opens the tense parts
chillness contracts the mass, enlarging
on it the water: one impulsion
with two effects on rock. The upright heaviness
will shift, snow stone and sky break
from each other. Here, the bridge is rock,
rock cut that cut stays as rock:
a curved stillness in air raised between two banks
of fanged rock eroded to sharpnesses.
                                        We cross Garva bridge,
the three stone arches subsumed
to what they are built in. The river
harshly slopes down over red shafts
of stone, milkishly tinged.
We tread in Wade's road, where other English
soldiers meticulously abandoned their minds
among rock, Scot, and revolt.

The mouthing shapes of red-dressed ferocity
stabbed, burned, and slit open what was there
until, by a stream spurting
into a crevice, then
scattering onto a shelf of rock, a dead man remains
who does not tend sheep, fence valley pasture
or grow to kiss his wife.

## *Opened*

Take from
me this ring
straightened open, a length
but, once,
contracted on your wrists.

love love: cries the
ring, straightened.

And again,
entering you.

What you have
taken off, you take
to you. The shaft:
the force,
reciprocally.

## *Our Selves*

My years compress in
to a man's substance.

Thirty years' space off, a domestic war's, I
rested in this street,
between my relative's sheets, a pupa,
my fierceness turned in on me, with a sting.
The soft insides outward facing.

My aunt died of a cancer, a replica
of her grating
through each tissue.
Her daughter is still
older than my self.

I don't know those who live
there now; I can't say to them:
I have recall here prior
to your strangeness to me.

The lips of the child I was stay
untouched: my years compress and harden.

Without fash, that is, your body admits me,
mine stiff with blood, its pressure
accumulating to its member

your menses distant
as the sun
is from the full moon.

Tenderness, with what draws my part into you,
hovers on your skin whose pores dilate, but as if each lived
a separate, identical life. A flower
opening out its particle of self, a female
pollen, rising to the surface for contact;
elsewhere the precise, heated focus of needs, softly rising
craves, insistent for the thing driven into you.

Strange, your own entity; distinct.
Your warmth
admitting mine.

A salted parsley; a sprig, musked and sharp.

## *Our Selves*

Without fash, your body admits me
mine stiff with blood, its pressure
accumulating to my penis

your menses distant
as the sun
from the full moon.

Tenderness, with what draws my part
into you, hovers within your skin. Its pores dilate
as if each lived a separate, identical life
like a flower rising, and opening its milky jot
at the skin, where there the threads of feeling
softly crave, insist for it to be driven in you.

My years compress to a man's substance.
The lips of the child remain untouched.

I rested between my relative's sheets
in a house close on yours. In that pupa
my fierceness turned in on me, and stung.

My aunt was fastened by a cancer, such replica
grating through each tissue, whose shape
of her she settled into. The kiss
dry on my skin, inlain, there, as if a trace
of white wood were chased into my substance
in the surface of a kiss
she drew herself into, I have put
in a box, with flints ignorant of friction.
That extended, that principal, Judaic phase
has left off. The candelabras
branch into some sort of magnificence.